conten

Modern baby knits by Alexa Ludeman & Emily Wessel

max & bodhi

Max is a monkey butt who enjoys stuffing whole bananas into his tiny gob, practicing high pitched screams at fancy restaurants, and pulling everything out of cupboards. He also loves to model knitwear, of course... But who wouldn't with that natural hipster hair?!

Bodhi a troublemaker who motors around at a mile a minute trying to keep up with her older sister and brother. She pretends to be one of the gang, throwing her head back to laugh like mama, even if she doesn't quite get the joke. Bodhi likes large carpeted expanses, free of toys, where she can practice her little bow legged steps.

baby knits

The last year was a productive one at Tin Can Knits! We survived one big book deadline, and added two new babies to our families. Max and Bodhi were born 6 weeks apart, and all Alexa and I could think about was the maximum cuteness potential of two babies in matching knits. This collection was simply unavoidable!

We think babies are hilarious. They often look like grouchy little old men, with balding heads, wrinkly skin, and adorable pot bellies! We love their silly giggles, diaper dances, and chunky thighs.

Inspired by our two newest darlings, this collection is filled with practical wardrobe staples. The designs are unisex because really, once the diaper goes on, so are babies! These tiny knits can be handed down from your sweet little squirrel to your sister's beloved peanut, or folded away as precious mementos of the baby days.

Nothing says love like a baby covered in woolies, so grab your needles, some lovely yarn, and cast on for a little cutie today!

Modern baby knits by Alexa Ludeman & Emily Wessel

Babies always need a classic cardigan in their wardrobe. They can wear it over a button down onesie for a semi-formal affair, or throw it on over a t-shirt for a casual tea party with friends!

playdate

a simple everyday cardi

materials:

Yarn: sock / fingering wt yarn - **refer to table (p8) for yardage**
(*samples shown in Sweet Fiber Cashmerino 20 in 'sea glass', 'canary' and 'spanish coin'*)

Needles: US #3 / 3.25mm and US #5 / 3.75 mm (*or as required to meet gauge*) circular and DPNs in each size
16" circular for small sizes, 24-32" for larger sizes

Gauge: 24 sts & 36 rows / 4" in stockinette on larger needles

Notions: stitch markers, darning needle, 5-13 buttons
approx 1/2" diameter

Modern baby knits by Alexa Ludeman & Emily Wessel

sizing: The pattern includes 8 child and 11 adult sizes.

Note: table lists finished garment measurements. Choose your size based on your measurements and desired ease.

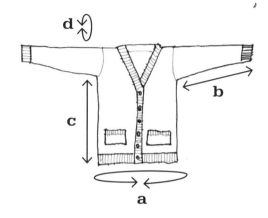

Size	Chest	Sleeve	Hem to Underarm	Upper Arm	Yard-age
0-3 mo	17"	7"	7"	6.5	300
3-6 mo	18"	7.5"	7.5"	7.5	350
6-12 mo	19"	8.5"	8"	8	400
1-2 yrs	21"	9.5"	9"	9	500
2-4 yrs	24"	11"	11"	10	650
4-6 yrs	26"	13"	13"	11	750
6-8 yrs	28"	15"	14"	12	900
8-10 yrs	29"	16"	15"	12	1000
Adult XS	31"	17"	16"	13	1150
S	35"	18"	17"	14	1300
SM	37"	18"	17"	15	1400
M	39"	19"	17"	16	1500
ML	41"	20"	17"	18	1600
L	43"	20"	18"	18	1700
LXL	45"	21"	18"	19	1800
XL	47"	21"	19"	19	1900
XXL	51"	21"	19"	20	2100
3XL	55"	22"	19"	20	2300
4XL	59"	22"	19"	20	2500

a chest / bust
b sleeve
c hem to underarm
d upper arm

sizing notes: This cardi looks best with 0-1" positive ease. Max and Bodhi are wearing size 3-6 mo with 1" positive ease. Lindsay is wearing the size S (35") with 0" ease.

pattern:

This cardigan is knit in one piece from hem to underarm, then fronts and back are separated and each is worked separately. Shoulder seams are joined and sleeves are picked up and worked to the cuff. Button bands are picked up and worked last.

pockets: *(make 2 the same)*

With larger needles cast on 16 (18, 20, 22, 24, 26, 26, 26, **30, 30, 32, 32, 32, 32, 34, 34, 36, 36, 36**) sts.

Work in stockinette *(knit 1 row, purl 1 row)* until piece measures 2 (2, 2, 3, 3, 3, 3, 3, **4, 4, 4, 4, 5, 5, 5, 5, 5, 5, 5**) inches, ending with a knit row. Place sts on hold.

body:

With smaller needles cast on 97 (103, 109, 119, 137, 149, 161, 167, **179, 203, 215, 227, 239, 251, 263, 275, 299, 323, 347**) sts.

Row 1 (RS): k2, [p1, k1] to last 3 sts, p1, k2
Row 2 (WS): p2, [k1, p1] to last 3 sts, k1, p2

Work in ribbing as established until piece measures 1 (1, 1, 1.5, 1.5, 1.5, 1.5, 1.5, **2, 2, 2, 2, 2, 2, 2, 2, 2, 2, 2**) inches from cast on, ending with a WS row. Change to larger needles.

Starting with a knit row (RS) work in stockinette *(knit 1 row, purl 1 row)* until piece measures 3.5 (3.5, 3.5, 4.5, 4.5, 4.5, 4.5, 4.5, **6, 6, 6, 6, 7, 7, 7, 7, 7, 7, 7**) inches from cast on, ending with a WS row.

place pockets:

Next row (RS): k5 (5, 5, 5, 6, 6, 8, 8, **8, 11, 11, 13, 15, 16, 17, 18, 20, 23, 26**) sts, PM,

[k1, p1] 8 (9, 10, 11, 12, 13, 13, 13, **15, 15, 16, 16, 16, 16, 17, 17, 18, 18, 18**) times, PM,

k55 (57, 59, 65, 77, 85, 93, 99, **103, 121, 129, 137, 145, 155, 163, 171, 187, 205, 223**) sts, PM,

[k1, p1] 8 (9, 10, 11, 12, 13, 13, 13, **15, 15, 16, 16, 16, 16, 17, 17, 18, 18, 18**) times, PM, knit to end

Pocket ribbing row 1 (WS): [purl to marker, rib to marker as established] twice, purl to end
Pocket ribbing row 2 (RS): [knit to marker, rib to marker as established] twice, knit to end

Work pocket ribbing rows 1-2 a total of 3 (**4**) times for child (**adult**) sizes, then work row 1 once more.

Next row (RS): [knit to marker, bind off to marker] twice, knit to end
Next row (WS): [purl to bound off sts, place held pocket sts from one pocket onto left needle, purl across them] twice, purl to end

Continue working in stockinette until piece measures 6 (6.5, 7, 8, 10, 12, 13, 14, **14, 15, 15, 15, 15, 16, 16, 17, 17, 17, 17**) inches from cast on, *(or 1 (2) inches short of desired length to underarm for child (adult) sizes)* ending with a WS row. Place a locking stitch marker in the work at the beginning and end of this row.

start neckline decreases:

Row 1 (RS): k2, ssk, knit to last 4 sts, k2tog, k2
Work 3 rows even in stockinette.

Work these 4 rows a total of 2 (**4**) times for child (**adult**) sizes. [93 (99, 105, 115, 133, 145, 157, 163, **171, 195, 207, 219, 231, 243, 255, 267, 291, 315, 339**) sts]

separate fronts and back:

Next row: k2, ssk, k14 (15, 17, 18, 22, 25, 28, 30, **31, 37, 39, 42, 45, 48, 50, 53, 59, 65, 71**) sts *(right front)*, bind off 6 (6, 6, 8, 8, 8, 8, 8, **8, 8, 10, 10, 10, 10, 12, 12, 12, 12, 12**) sts, *(1 st will be on your RH needle)*,

k44 (48, 50, 54, 64, 70, 76, 78, **84, 96, 100, 106, 112, 118, 122, 128, 140, 152, 164**) sts *(back)*,

bind off 6 (6, 6, 8, 8, 8, 8, 8, **8, 8, 10, 10, 10, 10, 12, 12, 12, 12, 12**) sts, knit to last 4 sts, k2tog, k2 *(left front)*

Your knitting is now separated into 3 sections: right front, back, and left front. Each section will be worked separately, then shoulder seams will be joined. Place sts for right front and back on hold and proceed to work left front.

left front:

WS will be facing.

Rows 1 and 3 (WS): purl
Row 2 (RS): knit
Row 4 (RS): knit to last 4 sts, k2tog, k2

Work these 4 rows until 14 (16, 16, 18, 20, 20, 22, 22, **24, 26, 28, 30, 32, 34, 36, 38, 42, 48, 54**) sts remain. Continue working in stockinette until piece measures 3 (3.5, 4, 4.5, 5, 5.5, 6, 6, **6.5, 7, 7.5, 8, 9, 9, 9.5, 9.5, 10, 10, 10**) inches from split, ending with a RS row. Break yarn leaving a long tail to work shoulder seam.

back:

With larger needles and WS facing, join new yarn. Work in stockinette until piece measures 3 (3.5, 4, 4.5, 5, 5.5, 6, 6, **6.5, 7, 7.5, 8, 9, 9, 9.5, 9.5, 10, 10, 10**) inches from split, ending with a WS row.

Next row: k14 (16, 16, 18, 20, 20, 22, 22, **24, 26, 28, 30, 32, 34, 36, 38, 42, 48, 54**), bind off 17 (17, 19, 19, 25, 31, 33, 35, **37, 45, 45, 47, 49, 51, 51, 53, 57, 57, 57**) sts, knit to end. Break yarn leaving a long tail to work seam.

right front:

With larger needles and WS facing, join new yarn.

Row 1 and 3 (WS): purl
Row 2 (RS): knit
Row 4 (RS): k2, ssk, knit to end

Work these 4 rows until 14 (16, 16, 18, 20, 20, 22, 22, **24, 26, 28, 30, 32, 34, 36, 38, 42, 48, 54**) sts remain. Continue working in stockinette until piece measures 3 (3.5, 4, 4.5, 5, 5.5, 6, 6, **6.5, 7, 7.5, 8, 9, 9, 9.5, 9.5, 10, 10, 10**) inches from split, ending with a RS row. Break yarn leaving a long tail to work shoulder seam.

join shoulder seams:

Join right front to right side of back and left front to left side of back using Kitchener stitch or 3-needle bind off. We used Kitchener stitch, however for more structure you may prefer to use a 3-needle bind off.

sleeves:

Sleeves are picked up and worked in the round to the cuff. With RS facing and larger needles, starting at the middle of bound off sts at underarm, pick up and knit 20 (22, 24, 27, 30, 33, 36, 36, **39, 42, 45, 48, 54, 54, 57, 57, 60, 60, 60**) sts to shoulder seam *(approximately 2 sts in every 3 rows)*, pick up and knit the same number back to center of underarm. Place BOR marker and join for working in the round.

[40 (44, 48, 54, 60, 66, 72, 72, **78, 84, 90, 96, 108, 108, 114, 114, 120, 120, 120**) sts]

Modern baby knits by Alexa Ludeman & Emily Wessel

Even on the best of playdates, it is only a matter of time before everyone's having a bit too much fun, things get rowdy, and the tears begin to flow!

Work in stockinette *(knit every round)* until sleeve measures 2 (2, 2, 2, 2, 1, 2, 3, **3, 2, 1, 2, 1, 1, 1, 2, 1, 3, 3**) inches from pick up.

Decrease round: k1, ssk, knit to last 3 sts, k2tog, k1   [2 sts dec]
Knit 5 (**4**) rounds for child (**adult**) sizes.

Work these 6 (**5**) rounds a total of 3 (5, 7, 9, 11, 14, 15, 15, **18, 20, 23, 24, 30, 29, 32, 30, 32, 28, 27**) times. [34 (34, 34, 36, 38, 38, 42, 42, **42, 44, 44, 48, 48, 50, 50, 54, 56, 64, 66**) sts]

Continue working in stockinette until sleeve measures 6 (6.5, 7.5, 8, 9.5, 11.5, 13.5, 14.5, **15, 16, 16, 17, 18, 18, 19, 19, 19, 20, 20**) inches *(or 1 (1, 1, 1.5, 1.5, 1.5, 1.5, 1.5, 2, 2, 2, 2, 2, 2, 2, 2, 2, 2, 2) inches short of desired length)*. Change to smaller needles.

Work in 1x1 rib *(k1, p1)* until cuff measures 1 (1, 1, 1.5, 1.5, 1.5, 1.5, 1.5, **2, 2, 2, 2, 2, 2, 2, 2, 2, 2, 2**) inches. Bind off all sts.

button bands:

With RS facing, using smaller needles, and starting at bottom right, pick up and knit approximately 4 sts in every 5 rows to first locking stitch marker, making sure to end with an even number of sts. Remove marker and place it on your needle.

Continue picking up at the same rate to the bound off sts at back neck, picking up an even number again. Pick up 17 (17, 19, 19, 25, 31, 33, 35, **37, 45, 45, 47, 49, 51, 51, 53, 57, 57, 57**) sts *(one in each bound off st)* at back neck. Pick up the same number as on right side to locking marker. Place the marker on your needles and

pick up the same number of sts down the left front as the right. There are an odd number of stitches in total.

Establish ribbing (WS): p2, [k1, p1] to last 3 sts, k1, p2

Continue ribbing as set (knitting the knits and purling the purls) for 2 (2, 2, 4, 4, 4, 4, 4, **4, 4, 4, 4, 4, 4, 4, 4, 4, 4, 4**) more rows.

Buttonhole row (RS): Work 5-13 two or three stitch buttonholes *(as described below)* evenly spaced to first marker, then rib to end **OR** rib to second marker then place buttonholes evenly to end

Two stitch buttonhole: sl 2 sts, pass the first over the second, sl 1 more st, pass the first over the second *(2 sts bound off)*. Slip 1 st from RH needle to LH needle, cast on 2 sts to RH needle

For a three stitch buttonhole, simply bind off then cast on 3 stitches in the same fashion.

Work a further 3 (3, 3, 5, 5, 5, 5, 5, **5, 5, 5, 5, 5, 5, 5, 5, 5, 5, 5**) rows in ribbing. Bind off all sts.

finishing:

Sew down the pockets, weave in all ends, sew on buttons corresponding to buttonholes.

Wet block your sweater and dress it up or down to look smart for your next playdate!

No matter how tiny they are now, one day they will grow up and fly away.

Inspired by flying geese quilt motifs, this modern geometric blanket is perfect for a new addition or a grown baby flying off to college.

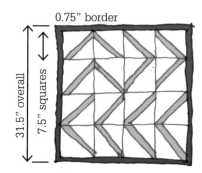

0.75" border

31.5" overall

7.5" squares

fly away

a bold and modern hand-knit quilt

sizing: Quilt blocks are approximately 7.5" square, and the border is 0.75" wide. The size is adjustable. The 16-square blanket shown measures approximately 31.5" square.

materials:

Yarn: DK weight yarn in MC and several CCs *(we used 8)*
per square: MC: 60 yds, CC: 20 yds
for 16 squares: MC: 960 yds, CCs: 320 yds total
plus 150 yds total edging *(sample uses 2 colours)*
*(Sample shown in Rainbow Heirloom Sweater
in 'almost spring', 'blue raspberry', 'fluffy bunny',
glowstick girl', 'jewel sea', 'koala haircut', 'natural',
'snow melt', and 'tidepool find')*

Needles: US#7 / 4.5mm *(or as required to meet gauge)*
straight or circular needles for blocks, 1-2 long
circular needles for edging

Gauge: 19 sts & 40 rows / 4" in garter stitch

Notions: stitch markers, darning needle

Modern baby knits by Alexa Ludeman & Emily Wessel

pattern:

This blanket is knit one square at a time. After squares are knit, they are seamed together. A border is worked around the edge to complete the project.

squares: Make each square the same.

Using MC, cast on 1 stitch *(simply place a slip knot over the needle)*. Leave a 20" long tail for seaming.

Row 1 (WS): kfb   [2 sts]
Row 2 (RS): kfb, k1   [3 sts]
Row 3: kfb, knit to end   [1 st inc]
Work last row 34 more times, until there are 38 sts.

Change to CC, leaving 6" long tails.

Row 38 (RS): kfb, knit to end   [1 st inc]
Work last row 11 more times, until there are 50 sts.

Change to MC.

Row 50 (RS): knit all stitches   [50 sts]
Row 51 (WS): ssk, knit to end   [1 st dec]
Repeat last row until 3 sts remain.

Next row (bind off): ssk, k1, lift first stitch over second and off needles. Break yarn, leaving a 20" long tail for seaming. Draw yarn tail through final stitch to complete the square.

Make as many squares as desired, using a combination of MC and CC colours per your design concept.

seaming:

Lay out the blanket squares in the desired configuration. Using yarn tails, sew squares together using mattress stitch, sewing through a purl bump on one side, then the corresponding purl bump on the other side, for a butted seam with minimal selvedge on the wrong side of the work. When you reach the CC stripes, it is neatest to seam these using the CC yarn tails.

edging:

To begin the edging you will pick up stitches, using a needle to pick up loops from the work itself, without the working yarn.

Starting at a corner, pick up one stitch right at the corner, then pick up 24 sts per square along the edge to the next corner *(approximately 1 st per 2 rows)*. *PM, then pick up 1 stitch right at the corner. Continue, picking up 24 sts per square along the next edge. Repeat from * until you have picked up at all 4 corners, and along all sides. Join edging yarn and knit 1 round. PM and join for working the in the round.

Note: because the blanket is quite large, you may need to use two circular needles in order to get all the stitches on the needles at once.

Increase round: [k1, (p4, m1p) to marker] repeat along all four sides of the blanket

This will increase the stitch count per square from 24 to 30 sts, so for a 16-square blanket, there are 30 x 16 = 480 sts. With the 4 corner sts there are 484 sts total for the edging. If you work more or less squares, the total edging stitch count will vary.

Round 1: [k1, m1, knit to last marker, m1, slip marker] repeat along all four sides of the blanket
Round 2: [k1, purl to marker, slip marker] repeat along all four sides of the blanket
Work rounds 1-2 a total of 2 times, then switch to another edging colour (if desired) and work rounds 1-2 once more. Bind off all stitches loosely.

finishing:

Weave in all ends and wet block blanket *(add white vinegar to wash water to prevent colours from running)*. Then snuggle up close with your sweeties before they fly away!

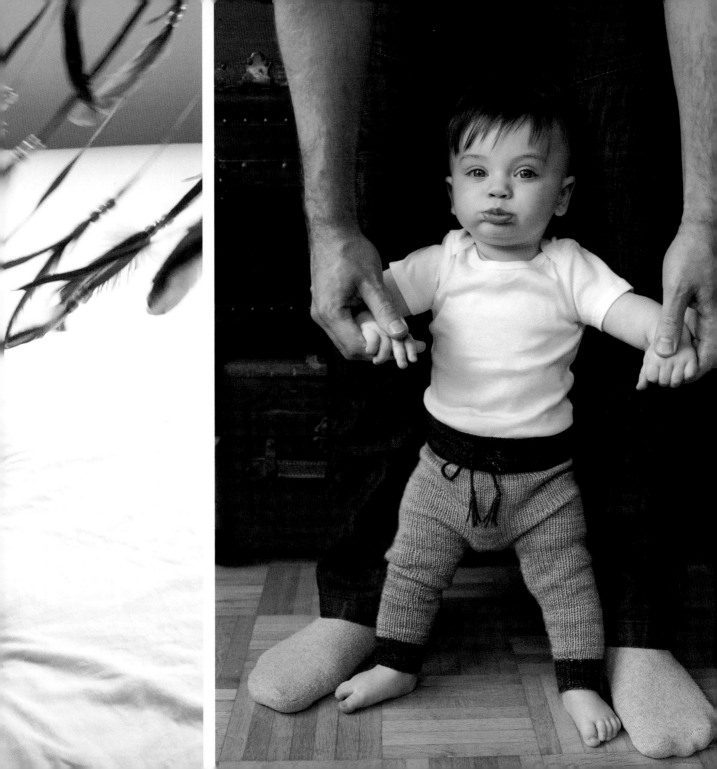

Left to their own devices, babies can get unaccountably chunky. Has your little darling just developed a third chin? Chubby little bracelets? Fat feet?!

If it's time for baby boot camp, then these joggers are just what your fitness-minded baby needs!

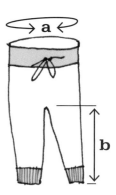

rocky

classic 80's joggers for the fitness–minded baby

sizing: 0-6 mo (6-12 mo, 12-24 mo)
finished measurements:
a) waist (unstretched): 15 (16, 17)"
b) leg (adjustable): 8 (9, 10.5)"

materials:

Yarn: sock / fingering weight yarn in one or two colours
single colour: 250 (300, 350) yards total **OR**
two colours: 140 (170, 200) yds MC plus
                        120 (135, 150) yds CC
*(Note: if you are adding an inch to accomodate
cloth diapers, add 30 yards) (samples shown in
SweetGeorgia CashLuxe Fine in 'bison', 'hush' and
'tumbled stone')*

Needles: US #1 / 2.25mm and US #4 / 3.5mm *(or as required
to meet gauge)* 16" circulars and DPNs

Gauge: 24 sts & 34 rounds / 4" in stockinette on larger needles
Notions: stitch markers, darning needle, spare circular

Modern baby knits by Alexa Ludeman & Emily Wessel

pattern:

These pants are knit from doubled waist band to cuffs with short row shaping to accommodate diaper bums. Pattern is written for 2 colours, if using a single colour simply ignore colour changes.

waistband:

Using CC and smaller needles cast on 102 (110, 118) sts provisionally, PM and join for working in the round.

Work in stockinette *(knit every round)* until piece measures 2.5 inches from cast on.

Next round: k21 (23, 25), yo, k2tog, k5, yo, k2tog, knit to end

Continue working in stockinette until piece measures 3.5 inches from cast on. Undo provisional cast-on and place sts on a spare needle. Fold the work in half, so that the newly added needle, with cast on sts, sits inside the needle with the working yarn.

Waistband joining round: with larger needles and MC, (k2tog) around, each time combining one st from the cast on and one st from work

Continue in stockinette until piece measures 2.5 (3, 3.5) inches from waistband join. *(Note: if your baby wears cloth diapers you may want to add an extra inch here)*

short rows:

Set up round: k51 (55, 59) sts, place SR (short row) marker, knit to end.
You will now have 2 markers, a BOR marker and a SR marker.

Short row 1: knit to last 8 sts, w&t
Short row 2: purl to 8 sts from SR marker, w&t
Next row: knit to end of round, picking up wrapped st and knitting it together with the st it wraps
Knit 3 rounds, picking up wrap and knitting it together with the st it wraps

Next short row: knit to last 10 sts, w&t
Next short row: purl to 10 sts from SR marker, w&t
Next row: knit to end of round, picking up wrapped st and knitting it together with the st it wraps
Knit 3 rounds, picking up wrap and knitting it together with the st it wraps

Next short row: knit to last 12 sts, w&t
Next short row: purl to 12 sts from SR marker, w&t
Next row: knit to end of round, picking up wrapped st and knitting it together with the st it wraps
Knit 3 rounds, picking up wrap and knitting it together with the st it wraps

Next short row: knit to last 14 sts, w&t
Next short row: purl to 14 sts from SR marker, w&t
Next row: knit to end of round, picking up wrapped st and knitting it together with the st it wraps
Knit 3 rounds, picking up wrap and knitting it together with the st it wraps

increases:

Round 1: k24 (26, 28), PM, m1, k3, m1, PM, k48 (52, 56), PM, m1, k3, m1, PM knit to end [4 sts inc]

Round 2: knit

Round 3: [knit to marker, SM, m1, knit to marker, m1, SM] twice, knit to end [4 sts inc]

Work rounds 2-3 a total of 3 (4, 5) times. There will be 11 (13, 15) sts between markers on each side [118 (130, 142) total sts]. Knit 1 round then proceed to separate for legs.

separate for legs:

Next round: knit to marker then break yarn leaving a 14" tail to work the crotch seam

Place 11 (13, 15) sts between front markers on spare needle, place leg sts to next marker on waste yarn *(these remain on hold until you are ready to work second leg)*, place 11 (13, 15) sts between back markers on spare needle.

With wrong sides together, graft the 11 (13, 15) sts from spare needles together using Kitchener stitch.

You will now have a seam at the crotch, 48 (52, 56) sts on your needle, and 48 (52, 56) sts on hold for second leg.

legs (work both the same):

With new yarn knit across 48 (52, 56) sts, pick up and knit 1 st from crotch, PM, pick up and knit 1 more st from crotch. Join for working in the round then knit to marker. [50 (54, 58) sts]

Knit 2 (4, 6) rounds.

Decrease round: k1, k2tog, knit to last 3 sts, ssk, k1 [2 sts dec]
Knit 4 rounds.

Work these last 5 rounds a total of 9 times. [32 (36, 40) sts]

Knit until leg measures 6.5 (7.5, 9) inches from separation *(or 1.5 inches short of desired length)*.

Change to smaller needles and work in 1x1 rib *(k1, p1)* for 1.5 inches. Bind off all sts loosely.

finishing:

To create braided ties cut 6 lengths of yarn, about 36 inches each. Braid these together.

To create i-cord ties use a DPN to cast on 3 sts. Knit 1 row. [Move all stitches to other end of needle, pull yarn tight across back of stitches, and knit another row] repeat until i-cord is 32", then draw yarn tail through remaining live stitches and secure.

Thread braid or i-cord through waistband holes.

Weave in ends and wet block pants. Put them on a cute little baby bum and admire!

Obviously when it comes to style, you want to give your baby the best possible start in life! This little hipster chic fair-isle vest is a must for going out to spoken word at coffeehouses, and gurgling... ironically.

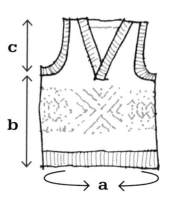

peanut

hipster chic fair-isle vest for your little peanut

sizing: 0-3 mo (3-6 mo, 6-12 mo, 1-2 yrs, 2-4 yrs)
a) finished chest: 18 (19.5, 21, 22.5, 24)"
b) hem to underarm length: 6 (6.5, 7, 8.5, 10)"
c) armhole depth: 3.25 (3.5, 4, 4.5, 5)"

materials:

Yarn: DK weight yarn in 2 colours
MC: 200 (230, 250, 300, 400) yds
CC: 60 (70, 80, 90, 100) yds
*(Samples shown in **The Uncommon Thread Merino DK** in 'seascape' with 'golden praline' and 'squirrel nutkin' with 'beeswax')*

Needles: US #4 / 3.5mm and US#6 / 4.0mm *(or as required to meet gauge)* 16" circular needle in both sizes, and DPNs in smaller size

Gauge: 22 sts & 28 rounds / 4" in stockinette on larger needles

Notions: stitch markers, darning needle

chart B: work rounds 1-25   **chart A:** work rounds 1-25

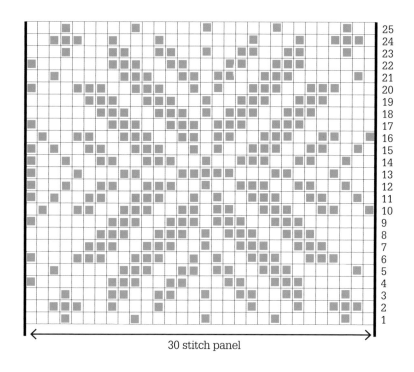

30 stitch panel

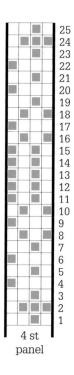

4 st
panel

key & abbreviations:

☐ **MC** - knit with main colour

▦ **CC** - knit with contrast colour

chart notes:

Charts are read from right to left.

Refer to text for how to locate charts.

Repeat chart A as many times as will fit between markers.

Chart B is worked once on the front and once on the back of the vest.

pattern:

This vest is knit in the round from hem to underarms. Fronts and back are worked in rows to the shoulders. Ribbed collar and armhole edgings are worked last.

body:

Using smaller needles and MC, cast on 100 (108, 116, 124, 132) sts, PM and join for working in the round. Work in 1x1 rib *(k1, p1)* for 1 (1, 1.25, 1.5, 2) inches. Change to larger needles and knit all rounds until work measures 1.5 (2, 2.5, 3.5, 4.5) inches from cast on. For a longer vest, add length here.

Set up round: k16 (16, 20, 24, 24), PM, k30, PM, k20 (24, 28, 32, 36), PM, k30, PM, knit 4 (8, 8, 8, 12) sts to end of round. These markers will define chart placement.

With MC and CC, work rounds 1-25 of charts: [Work chart A to marker, work chart B to next marker] twice, then work chart A to end.

Note: Your gauge in stranded knitting may be different from your stockinette gauge; if this is the case, use a larger needle for the stranded section, or knit with the work inside-out, drawing floats loosely across the back of the work. Take care to keep the CC yarn in the dominant position (always draw it up from beneath the MC yarn), as this will make the pattern 'pop'.

Remove all markers except beginning of round. With MC knit all rounds until work measures 6 (6.5, 7, 8.5, 10) inches from cast on.

Modern baby knits by Alexa Ludeman & Emily Wessel

split for fronts and back:

Remove BOR marker, knit 2 (0, 2, 3, 1) sts, bind off the next 7 (7, 7, 9, 9) sts *(left underarm)*, one st remains on RH needle, knit next 18 (20, 22, 22, 24) sts *(left front)*, bind off next 5 (5, 5, 7, 7) sts *(centre front)*, one st remains on RH needle, knit next 18 (20, 22, 22, 24) sts *(right front)*, bind off next 7 (7, 7, 9, 9) sts *(right underarm)*, one st remains on RH needle, knit to end *(back)*. [19 (21, 23, 23, 25) sts at left and right fronts, 43 (47, 51, 53, 57) at back]

Place left and right front sections on hold.

back: Back is worked in rows.

Next row (WS): purl

Row 1 (RS): k2, ssk, knit to last 4 sts, k2tog, k2 [2 sts dec]
Row 2 (WS): purl
Work rows 1-2 a total of 3 times.
[37 (41, 45, 47, 51) sts]

Continue knitting in stockinette until back measures 2.5 (2.75, 3.25, 4.25, 4.75) inches from underarm. Place the first and last 7 (8, 9, 10, 12) sts of the row on hold for the shoulder seams, and the central 23 (25, 27, 27, 27) sts on hold separately for the collar.

left front: Left front is worked in rows.
Attach MC yarn and begin with RS facing using larger needles.

Row 1 (RS): k2, ssk, knit to last 4 sts, k2tog, k2 [2 sts dec]
Row 2 (WS): purl
Work rows 1-2 a total of 3 times.
[13 (15, 17, 17, 19) sts]

Row 3 (RS): knit to last 4 sts, k2tog, k2 [1 st dec]
Row 4 (WS): purl
Work rows 3-4 a total of 8 (9, 10, 9, 9) times, until 5 (6, 7, 8, 10) sts remain.

Knit in stockinette until work measures 3.5 (3.75, 4.25, 4.75, 5.25) inches from underarm, ending with a WS row.

Row 5 (RS): knit to last 2 sts, m1, k2 [1 st inc]
Row 6 (WS): purl
Repeat rows 5-6 once more. [7 (8, 9, 10, 12) sts]

Place stitches on hold and break yarn, leaving a 12" tail for seaming.

right front: Right front is worked in rows.
Attach MC yarn and begin with RS facing using larger needles.

Row 1 (RS): k2, ssk, knit to last 4 sts, k2tog, k2 [2 sts dec]
Row 2 (WS): purl
Work rows 1-2 a total of 3 times. [13 (15, 17, 17, 19) sts]

Row 3 (RS): k2, ssk, knit to end [1 st dec]
Row 4 (WS): purl
Work rows 3-4 a total of 8 (9, 10, 9, 9) times, until 5 (6, 7, 8, 10) sts remain.

Knit in stockinette until work measures 3.5 (3.75, 4.25, 4.75, 5.25) inches from underarm, ending with a WS row.

Row 5 (RS): k2, m1, knit to end [1 st inc]
Row 6 (WS): purl
Repeat rows 5-6 once more. [7 (8, 9, 10, 12) sts]

Place stitches on hold and break yarn, leaving a 12" tail for seaming.

seam shoulders:

Seam fronts to back using either Kitchener stitch (grafting), or a 3-needle bind-off.

collar:

With RS facing, using smaller needles, attach MC yarn at centre front and pick up and knit at a rate of 4 sts in every 5 rows up the right front neckline to the held sts at back of neck. Knit across the 23 (25, 27, 27, 27) back of neck sts. Pick up and knit the same number down the left front neckline as at right, ending at the bound off sts at centre front. There should be an odd number of stitches. Do not pick up and knit in the stitches bound off at centre front.

Establish ribbing (WS): p2, [k1, p1] to last stitch, p1

Work a further 6 (6, 6, 8, 8) rows in ribbing as established, then bind off all stitches loosely. Overlap and sew down the collar to bound off sts at centre front of body.

armholes:

With RS facing and smaller needles, beginning at underarm, pick up and knit around the armhole at a rate of approximately 3 sts in every 4 rows, for a total even number of stitches. PM and join for working in the round. Work in 1x1 rib *(k1, p1)* for 4 rounds, then bind off all sts.

finishing:

Weave in ends, wet block the vest *(add white vinegar to wash water to prevent colours from running)* and dress up your little peanut!

Is there anything more delicious than baby feet? With their chubby little toes and soft skin, you just want to eat them right up.

To keep your little squirrel safe from hungry monsters who find baby feet irresistible, we recommend these cute and cozy socks!

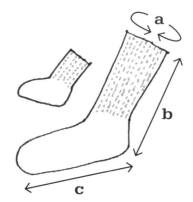

little squirrel

socks to keep a little squirrel snuggly and warm

sizing: newborn (baby, toddler, child, **adult S, M, L**)
finished measurements (unstretched):
a) cuff circumference: 4.25 (5, 5.75, 6.5, **7.25, 8, 8.75**)"
b) cuff length (adjustable): 4 (4, 6.5, 8, **9.5, 10.5, 11.5**)"
c) foot length (adjustable): 3.5 (4, 6, 7.5, **9, 10, 11.25**)"

materials:

Yarn: 75 (100, 125, 175, **200, 275, 300**) yds worsted / aran wt yarn
*(child and adult M samples shown in Hazel Knits
Cadence in 'lichen', 'frost', and 'white winged dove')*

Needles: US #5 / 3.75mm *(or as required to meet gauge)*
DPNs *(or circular for magic loop)*

Gauge: 22 sts and 30 rounds / 4" in stockinette

Notions: stitch markers, darning needle

Modern baby knits by Alexa Ludeman & Emily Wessel

pattern:

These socks are knit from cuff to toe.

cuff: Cast on 24 (28, 32, 36, **40, 44, 48**) sts, PM and join for working in the round.

Round 1: [k1, p1] around
Round 2: [k3, p1] around

Work rounds 1-2 until piece measures 4 (4, 6.5, 8, **9.5, 10.5, 11.5**) inches from cast on, ending with a round 2.

heel flap:

Next round: sl1, k11 (13, 15, 17, **19, 21, 23**), turn work

You work the heel flap in rows on these 12 (14, 16, 18, **20, 22, 24**) sts, all other sts are on hold.

Row 1 (WS): sl1, purl to end, turn work
Row 2 (RS): sl1, knit to end, turn work

Work rows 1 and 2 a total of 4 (4, 5, 6, **7, 8, 9**) times, then work row 1 once more. This will be a total of 10 (10, 12, 14, **16, 18, 20**) rows.

heel turn:

Row 1 (RS): sl1, k6 (6, 8, 10, **12, 12, 14**), ssk, k1, turn work
Row 2 (WS): sl1, p3 (1, 3, 5, **7, 5, 7**), p2tog, p1, turn work
Row 3: sl1, knit to 1 st before the gap, ssk, k1, turn work
Row 4: sl1, purl to 1 st before the gap, p2tog, p1, turn work

Newborn size only: knit across the remaining 8 sts and proceed to gusset & foot.

All other sizes: repeat rows 3-4 until all stitches have been worked: 8 (8, 10, 12, **14, 14, 16**) sts remain. Knit across these heel stitches.

gusset & foot:

Set up round: pick up and knit 6 (6, 7, 8, **9, 10, 11**) sts along the edge of heel flap, PM, k1, ssk, k6 (8, 10, 12, **14, 16, 18**), k2tog, k1, PM, pick up and knit 6 (6, 7, 8, **9, 10, 11**) sts along the edge of heel flap, k4 (4, 5, 6, **7, 7, 8**) sts, mark the new BOR (located in the middle of the bottom of the foot)   [30, (32, 38, 44, **50, 54, 60**) sts]

Round 1: knit
Round 2: knit to 3 sts before marker, k2tog, k1, knit to marker, k1, ssk, knit to end   [2 sts dec]

Work rounds 1-2 a total of 5 (4, 5, 6, **7, 7, 8**) times. [20 (24, 28, 32, **36, 40, 44**) sts]

Continue working in the round, knitting all sts until sock measures 3.25 (3.5, 5, 6.5, **7.5, 8.5, 9.75**) inches from back of heel or 0.25 (0.5, 1, 1, **1.5, 1.5, 1.5**) inches short of desired foot length.

toe:

To shift BOR remove marker, knit 5 (6, 7, 8, **9, 10, 11**) sts, then replace marker - this is the new BOR, located at the side of the toe.

Round 1: [k1, ssk, knit to 3 sts before marker, k2tog, k1] twice   [4 sts dec]
Round 2: knit

Work rounds 1-2 a total of 1 (2, 2, 2, **2, 2, 2**) times [16 (16, 20, 24, **28, 32, 36**) sts]. Then repeat round 1 until 12 (12, 12, 16, **16, 20, 20**) sts remain.

finishing:

Break yarn leaving a 12 inch tail, then graft
toe using Kitchener stitch. Put them on some
adorable baby feet or some chilly grown up feet!

Modern baby knits by Alexa Ludeman & Emily Wessel

'Put a hat on that baby!' curmudgeons would cry as my husband and I took our little one grocery shopping... in the middle of summer. Well this one's for you!

bumble

simple textured beanie for your little baby butthead

sizing: newborn (baby, toddler, child, **adult S/M, adult L**)
fits head 14 (16, 18, 19.5, **21, 23**)" around

materials:

Yarn: DK weight yarn in 1 or 2 colours
110 (130, 140, 150, **170, 190**) yds total
*(Samples shown in **Rainbow Heirloom Sweater** in
'boyfriend jeans' and 'cloudy sky', **The Uncommon
Thread Merino DK** in 'beeswax' and 'golden
praline' and 'toast' and 'squirrel nutkin', **Hazel
Knits Cadence** in 'frost' and 'white winged dove'
and **Sweet Fiber Merino Twist Worsted** in 'canary')*

Needles: US #5 / 3.75mm and US #10.5 / 6.5mm
(or as required to meet gauge) 16" circular needle
in both sizes, and DPNs in larger size

Gauge: 20 sts & 30 rounds / 4" in slipped stitch pattern
on larger needles

Notions: stitch markers, darning needle, pompom maker

Modern baby knits by Alexa Ludeman & Emily Wessel

Create different effects by using a single colour, 1-round or 2-round stripes. The wrong side has a beautiful texture too!

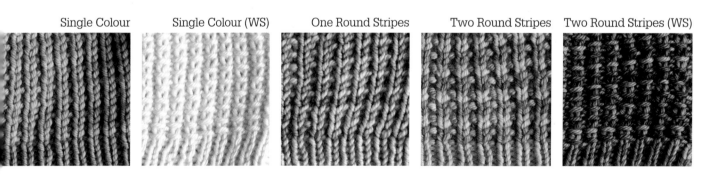

Single Colour | Single Colour (WS) | One Round Stripes | Two Round Stripes | Two Round Stripes (WS)

pattern:

Using smaller needles and MC, cast on 72 (80, 88, 96, **104, 112**) sts, PM, and join for working in the round. Work in 1x1 rib *(k1, p1)* for 7 (7, 9, 9, **11, 11**) rounds.

Switch to larger needles. For a 2-colour hat, change to CC. The slipped stitch pattern is a subtle tweedy check in 2 colours, a lovely waffle texture in a single colour, and also looks interesting on the reverse side, so you may prefer to wear your beanie inside-out!

For this pattern, all slipped stitches are slipped purlwise with yarn held in back.

Round 1:   [k1, sl1] around
Round 2:   [k1, p1] around

If working in 2-round stripes, work rounds 1-2 in CC, then 1-2 in MC, and repeat, continuing 2-round stripes for the rest of the project. For 1-round stripes, work round 1 in CC, and round 2 in MC, then continue working 1-round stripes for the rest of the project.

Continue in pattern until work measures 3.5 (3.75, 4, 4.25, **4.5, 4.75**) inches from cast on, ending with a round 1. For a slouchy hat, work 1-2 inches further before decreasing.

crown decreases:

If working a 2-colour hat, continue the stripe pattern as established throughout the decreases. Switch to DPNs when necessary.

Set up round: [(k1, p1) 9 (10, 11, 12, **13, 14**) times, PM] around

The markers divide the work into 4 sections, with 18 (20, 22, 24, **26, 28**) sts in each section.

Round 1: [ssk, (k1, sl1) to 4 sts before marker, k1, k2tog, sl1, slip marker] around   [8 sts dec]
Round 2: [k2, (p1, k1) to 2 sts before marker, k1, p1] around
Round 3: [ssk, (sl1, k1) to 4 sts before marker, sl1, k2tog, sl1, slip marker] around   [8 sts dec]
Round 4: [k1, p1] around

Work rounds 1-4 a total of 3 (3, 4, 4, **5, 5**) times [24 (32, 24, 32, **24, 32**) sts]. Work rounds 1-2 a further 0 (1, 0, 1, **0, 1**) times.
[24 sts, 6 in each section]

Next round: [ssk, k1, k2tog, k1] around   [16 sts]

Break yarn, thread yarn tail through remaining sts and pull tight to close top of hat. Make a pom pom and attach to top of hat.

Modern baby knits by Alexa Ludeman & Emily Wessel

Is this how you feel when you come up against a new knitting technique?

Don't be a baby! We've got some basic instructions in this section, but there are many more in-depth tutorials on our website:
www.tincanknits.com

techniques

blocking: Blocking is the final piece in any knitting puzzle. It radically improves most knitted projects by evening out the stitches, which is crucial for Fair Isle projects. To wet block, soak the finished knit in lukewarm water (adding a little white vinegar to prevent multi-colour projects from bleeding). Roll your knit in a towel, then stomp out the water. Finally, lay it out flat (or pin out) to dry.

charts: Each chart square represents a stitch as indicated by the key. Repeats are indicated by heavy lines, and are worked as many times as will fit in each round or row. Some charts illustrate every row (or round), and others illustrate only RS or odd numbered rows (or rounds), with the WS or even numbered rows or rounds described by text instructions. Always refer to chart notes and key before you begin.

Fair Isle / stranded knitting:
Stranded knitting uses two or more colours of yarn at a time to create multicoloured patterns. You knit a number of sts with one colour, then switch to the other colour, and knit a few more. The yarn not currently in use is carried loosely behind the work, creating 'floats'. It is important to relax and allow these floats to be very loose, so the fabric maintains elasticity and does not pull in too much. Another consideration when working stranded patterns is 'yarn dominance'. Essentially, the yarn that is brought up from underneath the other is more dominant and creates slightly larger and more 'dominant' stitches. When working a pattern, consider which colour you want to 'pop' more, and carry that yarn on the bottom consistently.

Modern baby knits by Alexa Ludeman & Emily Wessel

gauge: Gauge is a measurement of the size of the knit stitches. To knit a sweater that comes out the size you expect, you must begin by making a gauge swatch. Cast on 6 inches worth of stitches, and work in stockinette or the stitch stated in the gauge section until you have a 6 inch square. Wet-block the swatch and allow it to dry flat. Then measure the number of stitches and rows in a 4 inch square of fabric. If the gauge you have achieved in the swatch is more stitches than desired, the stitches are too small, so try again on larger needles. If the gauge is is less stitches than desired, the stitches are too big so try again on smaller needles, until you have achieved the pattern gauge.

kitchener stitch: Kitchener stitch, also known as 'grafting' or 'weaving' is a seamless method to join stitches. It essentially forms a new row in between two rows of live stitches. With a darning needle and yarn weave back and forth across the gap, maintaining the looping pattern of the knitted fabric.

pick up stitches: Using just the needle (without the working yarn), pick up a loop from the knitted fabric itself. On the following row (or round) you will use the working yarn and knit into this loop as if it were a regular stitch.

pick up and knit stitches: With RS facing, insert needle between sts (or rows), yarn over with working yarn on WS, and pull a loop through knitted fabric to RS (*one st picked up and knit*). Repeat until desired sts have been picked up and knit.

provisional cast on (crochet chain method): Using waste yarn, crochet a chain a few sts longer than you plan to cast on. With knitting needles and working yarn, insert needle under back bump of last crochet chain stitch. Yarn over and pull up a stitch. Continue along the crochet chain, creating as many sts as required. To 'unpick' the provisional cast on, unfasten the end of the crochet chain and it will 'unzip', leaving live sts ready to be worked.

put stitches on hold: Instead of binding off, thread a piece of waste yarn through the live stitches, so they don't unravel, and then remove the needles. You may alternately choose to use a stitch holder, but we generally suggest using waste yarn, as it is pliable and does not pull on the stitches.

short row shaping: To work short rows, you knit part of the way through a row, then stop and turn around before the end. Work as pattern specifies to the point where it says 'w&t' or 'wrap and turn'. This involves wrapping the working yarn around the next (unworked) stitch; bring yarn to front, slip next stitch from LH to RH needle, bring yarn to back, slip stitch back from RH to LH needle, then turn work. Proceed to work back in opposite direction. When the pattern says 'pick up wraps' this means you will work the wrap together (k2tog or p2tog) with the stitch it is wrapped around.

three-needle bind off: Place half the stitches on one needle, half on another. With right sides of work facing, use working yarn and a third needle to knit through one stitch on each needle at the same time. Repeat this, working a second stitch from each needle together. Lift the first stitch over the second and off the needle (one stitch bound off). Continue in this manner until all stitches have been worked together and bound off.

yarn substitutions: So much love and time goes into your knits, so spend the money on quality materials for best results. We recommend wool because is very forgiving (stretchy), can be blocked to adjust size, and makes for beautiful projects. For easy care we suggest machine-washable wools. Sock yarns are particularly well-suited to projects intended for babies; if held double a sock yarn can substitute for a worsted / aran weight yarn. Keep in mind that if you are making an adjustment to the pattern (adding length, width, pattern repeats etc) this will change your yardage requirements!

Modern baby knits by Alexa Ludeman & Emily Wessel

abbrev.

BOR beginning of round (marker)

CC contrast colour

dec decrease(d)

DPNs double pointed needles

inc increas(ed)

k knit

k2tog knit 2 stitches together

kfb knit into the front and back of one stitch

LH left hand

m1 make one knit stitch (any method)

m1p make one purl stitch (using LH needle, lift bar between sts, and purl through front loop)

MC main colour

p purl

p2tog purl 2 stitches together

PM place maker

RH right hand

RS right side of the work (public side)

sl slip one stitch (purlwise unless otherwise stated)

SM slip marker

ssk slip 2 stitches knitwise (one at a time), then knit 2 slipped stitches together through back loops

st(s) stitch(es)

w&t short row wrap & turn

WS wrong side of the work (private side)

yo yarn over (yarn forward / yfwd)

Modern baby knits by Alexa Ludeman & Emily Wessel

It's official: We love hand-dyes!

The exquisite palette we picked for Max & Bodhi's Wardrobe was created by these talented dyers. Thanks for contributing your colours to this book!

Hazel Knits
www.hazelknits.com

Rainbow Heirloom
www.rainbowheirloom.com

Sweet Fiber Yarns
www.sweetfiberyarns.com

SweetGeorgia Yarns
www.sweetgeorgiayarns.com

The Uncommon Thread
www.theuncommonthread.co.uk

thanks
Mom

Alexa and I both have tough, independent, badass Moms. And we both hope to be described in the same way once our kids learn to say 'badass'.

To Colleen: Thanks for showing me how to go my own way and be stubborn and pigheaded about it when necessary. Thanks for teaching me to love a great adventure. Finally, thanks for never letting me feel sorry for myself... even when a little bit of self-pity might have been justified! Love Emily

To Pat: Thanks for always supporting me in each of my endeavours. You have always been there with spot on advice, even when I wasn't smart enough to take it. Thanks for showing me that babies are hard to break, that they love going outdoors to run and play, and that you don't have to change who you are to be a good mom. Love Alexa

Modern baby knits by Alexa Ludeman & Emily Wessel

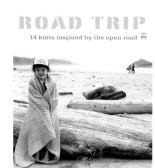    

Tin Can Knits: a creative partnership

We are Emily and Alexa, and we've been working hard to bring new knit designs (and new babies!) into the world for the past 5 years.

With an ocean between us, we knit and design for our families and for yours, creating patterns sized from baby to big. We have a modern style, and enjoy simple seamless constructions. We only bring you designs that we love knitting, and we are here to guide and support you, stitch by stitch.

Find in-depth tutorials on our website, and join us online to share your knits and stories.

www.tincanknits.com

max & bodhi's wardrobe

modern baby knits

by Alexa Ludeman and Emily Wessel
Tin Can Knits | www.tincanknits.com
Vancouver, Canada and Edinburgh, UK

To get your ecopy, go to
www.tincanknits.com/redeem
and enter this code:
4HBYQS8W